Transitory Moments

Poetry That Explores Impermanence

GAY GARLAND REED

Transitory Moments:
Poetry That Explores Impermanence
copyright © 2022 Gay Garland Reed

First Edition

ISBN-13: 978-1-945587-81-8
Library of Congress Control Number: 2022916547

1. Memories; 2. Buddhism; 3. Nature; 4. Spirituality

Book Design: Dancing Moon Press
Cover Design: Dancing Moon Press
Cover Art: Gay Garland Reed

Dancing Moon Press
Bend, Oregon USA
Lincoln City, Oregon USA
dancingmoonpress.com

DANCING
MOON
PRESS

For

My dear ones

Jeffrey, Heather & Alice

CONTENTS

Pondering Existence & States of Being   41

The endless knot, or eternal knot, appears in many cultures and religious traditions. In Buddhism it is one of the eight auspicious symbols and represents the union of wisdom and compassion. As you regard the twists and turns of the endless knot you are led to the realization that all things are endlessly transforming. Every moment is a transitory moment.

Processing Memories

THE MEMOIR WRITING CLASS

There are stories in that room
        stories that long to be heard

Stories of generosity and courage
        of generations of ancestors

Stories of regret, longing,
        loss of innocence

Stories that make us laugh, gasp,
        struggle to regain our balance

Stories that sit lightly
        and float in midair

And stories that bring on silence
        and a breathless stillness
        that no one dares to break

When I enter that room
        I surrender
        my anonymity

Sometimes I long to exit the entanglement
        of too many stories

but they hold me firm
        against my will
        riveted in the moment

In that room of endless stories
        we spill our truth and pain
                reliving the everyday
                        as art

Beyond Dissecting Memories

What are you up to?
Dissecting memories again?
       pulling them apart?
              examining their inner workings?

Not this time.
Today I'm pinning them to the board.
immobilizing them
       like exotic butterflies
              waiting to be admired
                   and cherished
                         for their rare beauty

One time I let them rip me apart
       cried them onto the page
              and felt ashamed

Another time I danced around them
       frantic
              ecstatic
              purging

Next week I will scrub them clean
       hang them on the line
              like Sunday laundry
       so the wind can whip around them
              wring them dry
              and the sun can bleach them white

Perhaps one day I'll
        sing those memories into the wind
                like Tibetan prayer flags
        blowing blessings
                into every corner of the universe

and then
        those memories
          like me
                will disappear
                        and join the Great Immensity

Encounters in Korea (1969-73): Memories from Peace Corps

Part 1
We arrived
cloaked in idealism
to wage peace
teach English
fight TB
How ignorant we were!

Sudden celebrities
Miguk saram, Miguk saram
(American! American!)
a gaggle of children
surround us
strangers in the "land of morning calm"

Along the street
a local Chinese medicine apothecary
Hanyak Bang
Glass jars filled with
preserved snakes
wooden drawers overflowing with herbs
horns, tusks of exotic animals,
sea creatures
we breathe in woody pungent
scents of cinnamon, star anise
bitter herbs for potent healing teas

In the countryside
following a mountain path through the forest
we meet three gray-robed Buddhist nuns
shaven heads, bright-eyed, curious
We are lured up the mountain by the beat of a
wooden *mok-tak* (wooden bell and mallet)
heartbeat of the mountain
dissolving into chant
as we near the temple
Namu Abitabul, Namu Abitabul

On a day in fall
cartloads, mountains of cabbage
fill the streets
preparing for *kim jiang*
kimchee making time
Ajumoni's fingers scarlet
raw from mixing hot pepper and garlic
grating radishes
cutting, washing, salting cabbages
preparing for winter.

Beside the sea
tingling salt spray
mingles with fishy smells
clotheslines hung with cuttlefish
drying in the sun
tentacles stiff

Returning to my
Hasook chip
one evening
Shocked
to see a blonde foreigner
at the end of the hall
My own refection in the mirror

Part 2

Raw, refined,
        blatant, nuanced
                pungent, acrid
Frigid outside
        in blustery January's
        breathlessly icy wind
        slicing through the paper windows

Blistering hot inside
        on charcoal heated *ondol* floors
        under the thick cotton *ibul* quilt

Large brown *kimchee* jars lined up
        beside the mud and wooden house
        a shiny crockery army
        guarding against hunger

in the sepia winter landscape
        empty rice fields
        thick rice-straw roofs
        ice puddles and pathways

One frozen coral persimmon
        too high to reach
        atop a barren branch
        a singular point of color in the beige
        landscape

As spring arrives
on the mountainside
beside a stream
raucous grandmothers
smoking, singing, dancing away their cares
invite this stranger to join in
they pull my blonde hair
hard
to see if it is real
laugh in satisfaction

their first encounter with a foreigner

A long Journey to Buddhism

It began over 50 years ago
this attraction.
It may have been in the shadow of
the great *Kamakura Daibutsu's*
serene in stillness
compassion

Or in the sand and rock
Zen garden
of *Ryoanji*
temple

Along the way
in the sometimes quiet
sometimes bustling
temples of
China, Korea, Japan, Thailand, Sri Lanka,
Nepal and Bhutan
it crept into my being

I learned to ride the breath
quietly
sometimes fitfully
into meditation
taming the frenetic mind

almost
Stirred by mesmerizing chants
rhythmic beats of the wooden
moktak bell
mimicking heartbeats
intoxicating incense
ornate *tankas* and *mandalas*
feeding all the senses

Moving toward emptiness
fullness
spaciousness

it arrived gently

like drinking tea

in tiny sips

over many ages

in many places

I allow the warm
fragrant solution
to penetrate
heal

Dissolve the icy notion of
original sin
in favor of
potential bliss

Bodhisattva grace
androgynous
both/and
giving
receiving
loving kindness
spiritual sustenance

Immutable Memories

Caulking around the edges of the moment
so none of its magic
could escape
I sealed it in

Or so I thought

But even indelible memories
are written in disappearing ink
after all

Memories are shapeshifters
bending and transforming
in unexpected ways
like photographs
cryogenic images
frozen in time
Or so I thought

But when I look again
later
the image morphs

The cast is the same
but they appear in different guises
and disguises

It was a happy family
Or was it?
It was a joyous day
Or was it?
Immutable memories
mutable
after all

MY BETTER HALF

He arrived the day after Christmas in 2002.
        a tiny pup
                barely eight weeks old

He came to Oahu from the Big Island
        in someone's pocket.
Because he's part Tibetan Spaniel,
        we called him Lama,
        knowing he would be our teacher.
Because he's part Chihuahua,
        I sometimes whisper "Fernando Lama".
He doesn't get the joke,
        but that's okay.
                I laugh at my own joke
                    and he's content.

In the early years he chased crabs
        at Swansea beach
        darted up the cliffs
        at Crouching Lion in Ka'a'awa.

He had his moments of fame
        in the Hawai`i state legislature
                doing his "Lama" thing,
        reminding the harried legislators to breathe.
A parade of admirers came to visit him
        bringing treats and their frustrations.

"Business at the legislature never ran more smoothly",
          one senator said.

Years later
          he's losing his hearing.
                    So am I.
His eyesight is going.
                    So is mine.
We're aging in tandem,
                    he and I.
While we lose our faculties
          the bond between us
                    never falters.

Like old friends,
          we read each other's minds.

Today, at almost 15,
          he walks in front of me

his tail a metronome,
          swinging
                    back and forth
                              marking time

He's the half of my soul that wags its tail.

No other explanation

Strangely familiar
       the mesmerizing meditation
       of grinding the ink stick
       with water on a carved stone

       Round and around
       back and forth
       trance-like
       dissolving time

Smooth sweet incense scent of black ink
       and pristine whiteness of
       tissue thin paper

Black and white
       ultimate contrast
       perfect complements

Lifting the bamboo and rabbit hair brush
       I dip it into the thick dark fragrant ink
       and prepare to press my spirit onto the paper

Writing Chinese characters
       so novel
       and yet so familiar
       that I believed
       that I was Chinese
       in another lifetime

FAREWELL CALIFORNIA

(Inspired by William Falkner: "The past is
never dead; it's not even past.")

When she left she imagined that it would disappear,
that place where she had first seen a robin
felt the alligator skin of an avocado
and reached between the branches of a tree
to pick an orange

When she crossed over that immense bridge
on her way to Somewhere else
she imagined that the orange trees
and avocado trees
would disappear

Even before she said farewell,
she had already mourned their absence a thousand
times
"They will be gone", she thought.

Now,
sometimes,
in the silent moments of Somewhere else

she returns
crosses the bridge
feels the alligator avocado skin

reaches for the orange
amidst the branches

In those moments she knows that
places burrow into our bones
they are always there
waiting to be reincarnated
in memories.

Reveling in the Mysteries of Nature

TREE-LIKE

She became more tree-like
as she aged
her hands wrinkled & gnarled
mottled & brownish
bark-like
an etched narrative
a scrimshaw tale
of hours turned to days
turned to decades

And beneath the topsoil
she became more tree-like
as she aged
beyond the view and ken of those
who lived on the surface
she reached out
extended
her roots long and deep
connecting
invisibly
with other tree-like souls
sought
the hidden spaces of existence
that she had not understood when she
strutted along manicured pathways
among the visible
fancying herself untethered

Now she's learning a new language
that dismantles "I", "me", "my"
in favor of dense
networks of connection
lacy webs of mycological consciousness
communicating silently
below the surface
out of sight
and the ken
of beings who live
above

QUEEN ANNE'S LACE

When Queen Anne's Lace,
in all its delicate grace,
appears along the roadside
we know that
            we are sliding
                        down the back of summer

Cloud-wisp Patterns

This morning I greeted a tie-dye sky
Clouds were streaks of white against a pale indigo
backdrop
as if someone had bunched up the sky in the corner
of the universe
and dipped it in pale indigo dye

Birds Filibustering

Birds filibustering
cooing, chattering
squawking, sputtering
languages rough and guttural
sweet and lilting

cacophony invades
the morning stillness

Hummingbirds in the snow

The winter landscape is in gentle animation.
a quiet snowfall backdrop
to a frenzied dance

Five crazed hummingbirds compete
for four plastic flowers on the feeder

It could be speed skating
or roller derby
or the Indianapolis 500
out there on the deck

Five tiny Shivas
Five dizzying dervishes
dancing
delighting this old woman

and the snow falls softly

HUMMINGBIRD COMFORT

She pauses on a skinny branch
of Japanese Snowbell
where the first traces of spring green
emerge

From this perch
she has a clear view of the feeder
that tempts her with its red plastic flowers
and C & H sugar water

She is my companion
my delight
during this time of isolation

An epic battle at my kitchen table

Early February inevitably hatches a curious dilemma.
a grand battle
Not a skirmish between pancakes and scramble
or Oolong and Earl Grey
It's more consequential than that.

The essential question is:
Should I wade through the pile of paper
        to begin income taxes?
or
        succumb to the allure of the Whole Seed
Catalogue
        and allow myself to dream of a spring garden?

How can the mundane world of
gross payments and total deductions
compete with visions of
        Brad's atomic grape tomatoes and
                Hill Country heirloom okra?

Why would I fret over property assessments
        and Required Minimum Distributions
when I could be salivating at the thought of harvesting
        Molokai purple sweet potatoes and
                Rajasthan honey melons?

Their exotic names alone
        transport me
        to verdant spaces
        that melt the February chill.

Adding, Subtracting,
        columns and rows,
One option diminishes me
        the other enlivens my spirit
One in black and white
        the other a riot of vibrant delight

If only all battles had such clear winners and losers.

Harvesting tomatoes and cavorting with a goddess

There is an astringent
slightly spicy tang in the air.
Breathe in that unmistakable tomato scent!
On a scorching summer's day
there's nothing like it.

Cherokee purple, True black brandywine,
Green zebra, Japanese black trifele,
Brad's cosmic grape, Bulgarian pink
grown from heirloom seeds
gathered and passed along by
organic farmers, grandmothers, veteran seed savers

We touch the thick leather-like
reptilian leaves
the scent of tomato foliage
lingers on our fingers.
These tangled bushes
their multiple arms akimbo like a Hindu goddess
Bhuvaneshvari, Mother of all Worlds,
beckoning from another realm

We are lured into their hidden spaces
in search of bounty
In an hour we haul a galactic
pile of saffron, crimson, green striped,
maroon and purple fruit into the kitchen
where empty jars wait patiently
for us to do our work

Someday when we are deep into winter
after days of dreary sunless skies
we'll open a jar of those tomatoes
and be transported
back into the arms of Bhuvaneshevari
smell her scent on our fingertips
feel the warmth of the sun on our backs

PINK RAIN, PINK TEARS

It's raining pink
I used to think
as the spring breezes
and gravity
pushed and pulled
the rosy petals from
the ornamental plum across the street

Careening
scuttling across the road
puddling along the sidewalk
like heavy rain

Now, it isn't pink rain I see
but tears
this ornamental plum is
weeping pink

It happened this morning
after the truck pulled up
and released its assassins.

A raging chain saw split open
the morning silence
its jagged teeth
reduced the plum around the corner
in minutes
to a pile of sawdust.

Did my steadfast tree
hear the screeching saws
or did she get the message
like Morse code through her roots
when the tree down the street
sent out its dying wail?

SUNLIGHT

There is a fulsome gorgeousness about the sunlight
       that pours through the window
       puddles on the kitchen floor

As afternoon proceeds
       it creeps across the floorboards
       spreading golden
           like rich olive oil

Thick
       viscous
           like sticky honey
it makes a slow procession
       across the room
wending its way
       like a caravan of camels
           through the vastness
               of the Gobi desert

Fireweed Puff

sometime around the beginning of August
when the air is parched
fireweed sends out its puffs
little parachutes that hold the promise
of purply-pink flowers next year

they float horizontal
animating the weighty stillness
of a summer's day

then vertical
when a gust
helicopters them skyward

between the wide slats on the deck
one is caught in a spider web
it boogie-woogies in the wind
wriggling like a captured insect
sits still when the breeze recedes

Does the spider mistake it for a fly?
perhaps

it is this way
things that seem to be one thing
are really something else

Pondering Existence & States of Being

NO NOTHING

There is no Nothing
There is always Something
When this Somethingness dissolves
there will still be Something
Something else
Something different
That's the law of physics

So when we suffer loss
It is really only Change
Change from something
to something else
That's the law of Nature

The pieces of that Somethingness
have become Something else
Look for it among the leaves
or in the soil
or flying in the sky overhead
Listen for it in the wind
Smell its subtle fragrance in an apple blossom
Taste its arresting essence in a basil leaf

There is no Nothing
There is always Something
Even emptiness is Something
That's the law of Existence.

One Exquisite Moment

one exquisite moment in the day
when you are fully present
with a flower or a friend

when you abide in the contours
of that moment
so deeply that you can feel it sculpting
you heart

THAT SILENCE

that silence that

laces things together

holds them in place

for an instant

long enough

for luminous listening

that silence

clears a space for

growing a soul

Co-creation

an idea sits between us
not yours, not mine
suspended in midair
it floats

our imaginations & conversations
push it back and forth
like a balloon
nudging it
higher & wider

forming & reforming
we reign it in
like a wild mustang
or let it burst
like a dandelion puff
spreading its seeds

both yours & mine
a product of our synergy
our shared breath
we grow it together

WHEN THE WORLD CLOSES IN

There are days when the world is too close
            when it closes in
                        and eats me alive

days when I think I can't breathe
                        and my body doesn't want to

days when the panic is so real
            that I'm sure there is a monster
                        over my shoulder

Despair has a face
            and it is staring me down.

On those days
            I look to the sky
            to the stars
where there are worlds
            beyond worlds
universes beyond universes
            billions and trillions of them
                        and more beyond

On those days
      I know that the world that is
      that is closing in on me
      stealing my hope
      is but a speck of dust
      that I can brush away
          render impotent
            with a thought

I look to the stars

GRIEF SOMETIMES VISITS LATE

Long after the goodbyes
    the tears
        the pats on the back that let you know
           you are not alone
It happens

Sometimes when you are almost sure
    that you are past the sadness
        when everyone else has
        almost forgotten

it sets you spinning
    carries you away in a flash flood

Sometimes grief creeps up unexpectedly
    out of the quiet depths
        and twists your heart

Sometimes amidst the most mundane routine
    Sometimes when you least expect it
        your everydayness
           is shattered by an
        overwhelming
             moment of
          remembering
Sometimes grief visits late

The nature of Wisdom

wisdom begins in droplets
in dribs and drabs
and builds
an ocean

in the realm of wisdom there are no gushers
only uncoverings
gradual revelations
through the marination of time

wisdom
slow like treacle
makes a late entrance
with the pile on of days

as wisdom grows
the labyrinth of information
the bits and pieces of existence
rearrange
conjoin
to reveal "the pattern that connects"*

that wisdom lives deep in the marrow
knows the terrain of silence
listens
to the quiet voice of the universe.

(*Gregory Bateson)

Ripening Awareness

Somehow she thought that awareness
would appear
like a fairy godmother
or a fiery comet
lighting up the night sky

she thought it would be sudden and intense
and leave no residue of doubt or confusion
it would be pristine and perfect
with no going back

But it didn't happen that way
It came like a slow sunrise
dawning silently without fanfare
like the ripening of a mango turning
from green to golden to rosy
It crept in quietly
like the gradual awakening from a deep sleep

It is still tentative, unfinished
but in the eloquence of silence
she apprehends its unfolding

is aware
of being aware

Pleating existence

One day she realized that today
      was like yesterday
           and the day before

"Life is a neatly
      pleated skirt of existence",
      she thought.

each pleat perfectly uniform
      folded back upon itself
           starched and pressed
      like the one before
           and the one after
              and the one after that

together they stretch into an accordion
      that plays sad tunes
           and lamentations
           from far off countries

"How did it become this way?" she wondered.

Messenger

Steel tongue drum vibrates me gently
into the new year
Her mandala face a primal circle of life
and death
whispers of infinity

Mallets kindle
        her heartbeat
her vibrant voice
        breathes the story of the universe
her tones stir memories of
        Indonesian *gamelon*
        native flutes
        sacred chants
On this morning of the new year
        and decade
I invite her spirit to
        resonate,
        to awaken me.
She is a messenger
who speaks to me in many tongues
entreating me to enter her world
igniting a meditation of possibility,
reconciliation,
compassion
and light.

Writing poetry in the time of COVID-19

Picking up the pen I'm on the edge of a precipice
looking over a vast empty desert
bereft

a barren landscape
no fertile soil for inspiration to grow
just patches of crusty dry cracked earth
parched

engulfed in silence
great ravines of silence
I call out to the darkness
but there is no response
not even a weak echo
thoughts, ideas have fled
leaving me destitute
I feel the vastness of my isolation

inspiration has gone underground
entrapped like Persephone
hibernating in some cave
out of sight
Or perhaps lurking in the depths of my being?
A delusion?
the reflection of a tangled self?

Another way to love the world

After a hiatus of a few decades
I took up the pencil
and began to draw

Close
careful observation
attending to form
to shadow
light

I made a pact with the paper

Let the image emerge and
I will coax it along
with whatever
worn out skills
I can muster or hone

Time went by
I was absorbed

A romance developed
and slowly
I realized that I had discovered
another way to love the world

An artist's challenge

Today I tried to
capture the soul of water

the way that water droplets
shiver on a leaf

round, robust
bursting with light

I wondered,
Could I ensnare
their luminescence
their translucence
with a pencil
or charcoal?

Rapt

wrapped in silence

rapt in silence

contemplating the vastness

between atoms and molecules

contemplating the vastness

between stars and universes

contemplating the stillness

between

inculcating these wonders
into every cell of your being

until they release a flow
of images
of words

how remarkable to live in a world
inoculated with such wonder

even for a moment

In a Trance

Floating untethered
      shot through with
           slices of sunlight

In the dew spangled morning
      I see melting diamonds

In the deafening quiet
      I hear the crunch of sand
          beneath my feet
taste the stinging saltine air
      yet float above the waves
      until mother returns from death
      to retrieve me
She
      with her infinite enthusiasm for a leaf
      is adrift
      in this landscape of sand and salt.

Two faces of solitude

Sometimes the solitude of "I"
        weighs down on me
and I envy those
        who speak in "we"

In those moments when solitude
        triggers longing
        for unfulfilled relationships
and harbors regrets
        for untested love
solitude is an unrelenting ache
        a chasm of loneliness.

But it need not be this way!

I could dive into
        the spacious moment of solitude
and find the pure
        contentment of connection
        to every sentient being and
        inanimate stone

Solitude could be an opening
        a conduit for unobstructed joy
        a pathway to the depths of a soul.

Spaciousness

Spaciousness

        spiritual generosity

openness

    acceptance

        field of endless possibility

emergent

    reaching inward

        stretching outward

    ever unfolding

Spaciousness

    a sacred state

WORSHIP

I tiptoe into the sacred space of your existence
Will you let me enter?
Should I prostrate myself before you
like a Tibetan devotee
before the image of Buddha?

Should I perform a ritual?
Pledge my devotion?
Walk the
elaborate labyrinth
of adoration?
recite mantras?

Or can we sit as equals
across the table from each other
sipping cups of lemon verbena tea
and sharing our stories?

Existence

(You exist as an idea in your mind.
~Shunryu Suzuki)

I am a thought
Sometimes your thought
Sometimes mine

Sometimes I'm a momentary thought

     Sometimes a lingering thought

       Sometimes a profound thought

         Sometimes a passing thought

         Occasionally, a pregnant
   thought.
One day,
   I'll become
     an afterthought.

Poetry in the Community

Four of the poems in this volume have been part of poetry projects in the community of Vancouver, WA that work toward integrating poetry into everyday life.

Before the pandemic, the Vancouver Public Library put out a call to writers and visual artists in 2019 to submit a work for a project called Visions and Voices. I submitted my poem, "Beyond dissecting memories", and it was chosen to be part of the project. The art team at the library sent my poem to a visual artist who painted a picture based on the poem and I was sent her painting, "Farewell California", that inspired me to write the poem of the same name in this volume. After nearly a year delay due to COVID-19, the Visions and Voices Exhibit went on display at the main branch of the Vancouver Public Library in November and December of 2021.

Two other poems were part of Poetry Moves, a program of Artstra, a nonprofit arts advocacy group in southwest Washington that collaborates with C-Tran to provide poetry on bus channel cards in all C-Tran buses. Ten new poems by local and regional poets or student poets are chosen from many entries and are installed on buses every six months. "Queen Anne's Lace" and "Tie-dye sky" were chosen in 2019 and 2020 to be part of this program.

Acknowledgements

It could have been such a lonely path, this journey of introspection and remembering, but it wasn't. The solitude of writing was alleviated by generous friends and fellow writers who have taken the time to read my work and offer comments. In particular, I have gained so much from my three long-term writing compatriots, Joanne, Judy and Sally, whose insightful comments and suggestions have spurred me to review and revise for many years, first in Hawai`i, and now in the Pacific Northwest. I offer abundant gratitude to them and to all of the many people who read my first little chapbook, Dragonfly Spirit, and encouraged me to keep writing. Among that group are the wonderful writers who attended Christopher Luna's memoir class. Finally, I want to thank Kim and Todd at Dancing Moon Press whose skills and expertise have helped to bring this work into being.

DANCING
MOON
PRESS